TORI TE

Conversations
with Alzheimer's

Advice on Life, Love, and Aging
From Those With
Alzheimer's and Dementia

Cover design by Kerry Hardin

Illustrations by Tori Tellem

Book design by Oana Rafaila

Comfort Human™ is a registered trademark with the United States Patent and Trademark Office

Library of Congress Control Number: 2021904657

Printed in the United States of America

For Anne Tellem and Bea Collins
Thank you for teaching me
how to have conversations.

CONTENTS

Introduction

My grandmother died suddenly. It feels weird to say "suddenly," considering she was 97.

She had been living at a wonderful nursing-home facility at the time of her death. She had aged through its various levels of care, first in independent living, then dying in the memory-care unit. Changing her life by moving to this community wasn't a decision the family had to make on her behalf. She called around to find a living situation and made the financial and other arrangements all on her own, then informed us of her new address. First and foremost, she looked forward to not having to cook and clean anymore. During the first month, she said it felt like a vacation. There was a nurses' station in her building to keep track of medication and doctors' appointments, but otherwise, they were hands off and Grandma was free to be.

That meant she could leave the premises to join organized group field trips or to take long walks by herself in the surrounding neighborhood whenever the mood struck, just as she had been while living alone in her apartment in Southern California. This was her life for a couple years.

One day, my dad called me. "She wanted to take a walk and went so far she couldn't get back." That was Grandma—in her 90s and still walking for miles on end, immersed in the scenery and people-watching. The problem wasn't the distance, though. She had knocked on the door of a random house and told the owner she couldn't remember where she lived.

Although her memory issues were still considered minor, the facility and my family agreed she should be moved to the next level of care. Unfortunately, there were no rooms available. The only vacant space they could find for her was within the Alzheimer's/dementia memory-care unit, a building with entry and exit under lock and key, a common safety practice with that kind of residency. She was still very lucid, so it was a tough change, especially with the loss of some freedom and no longer having anyone around her that she could have deep conversations with. However, she was granted permission to continue her solo walks, just as long as she didn't leave the property. She understood.

Then things shifted again. She was having more memory issues as well as delusional thoughts, such as calling my father to say she'd fallen in love and was getting married, or to report in hushed tones that her roommate—or the staff—was plotting to kill her.

I also started to see changes during our weekly visits. For example, she would greet me at every visit with, "Have you been away?" Believing more time had passed than actually had caused her to be sad at the end of our visits, as she couldn't retain that I'd return again the following week. The only "solution" I could come up with was to say, "See you in a couple days." I knew in my heart she wouldn't remember me saying that, but selfishly it eased my guilt of knowing she'd feel abandoned. Eventually, my parting words graduated to a fib: "I'm going to the bathroom." To me, that sounded like I'd be right back. I figured—hoped?—that while I was in the "bathroom," she'd forget I'd ever been there, thereby eliminating the difficulty of watching me leave the building and feeling any associated sadness or loneliness.

As her dementia progressed, she would sleep through our visits, so I took the opportunity to chat with other Alzheimer's/dementia residents who lived on her same floor. One in particular enjoyed pop culture and trashy entertainment magazines, and she was snarky with a hearty laugh. We could spend a solid hour talking nonstop. After a few weeks, she called me her "friend" and I felt the same. She was one of the lucky ones; her family visited often and brought her to their home for holidays and special occasions. They also supplied her with plenty to read and do. I'll never forget the hilarious time we had building and decorating—and eating—a gingerbread house together.

This same special friend was astute enough to notice I was now visiting my grandmother much more often because of her rapidly deteriorating health, and therefore she kept her jokes to a respectful minimum. This same caring friend sat in a chair outside my grandmother's room and quietly watched over me, doing the same to my grandmother when I wasn't there. And in the final minutes of my grandmother's life, as I held her hand as she took her last breath, this same loyal friend paced in the hallway with concern, her oxygen tank trailing behind.

After my grandmother was put in care of the mortuary, I stayed behind to pack up a few belongings and to find a dress for her to be buried in. When I left her room for the final time, I had 97 years of life in my hands, fitting in a single box. I entered the "living room" of the second floor of the memory-care unit that had been the final place my grandmother called home and found myself unable to leave. My grandmother's "neighbors" in each room of each wing had become a huge part of my life. It was then that my special, caring, loyal friend joined me. We hugged. "Are you leaving?" she asked. I looked at her for a moment. "I'm going to the bathroom," I replied. And that same day, I became a decades-long volunteer.

I made the decision immediately after my grandmother died that my life's mission would be to improve the mental health of those living with Alzheimer's/dementia and to those in hospice. I made the decision that I would do everything I could to ensure no one with Alzheimer's/dementia felt alone. I made the decision that whenever possible, I would make sure no one with Alzheimer's/dementia died alone, determined to sit vigil with them in their final hours, even if that was the first time we ever met.

It also became the motivation behind why I launched Comfort Human™. The name was inspired after I did a curiosity-based online search one day. Emotional-support animals have legitimate therapeutic effects for various conditions, such as anxiety and autism. But at that moment in time, many people were taking advantage of this, bringing their non-service dogs—aka their regular pets—with them everywhere under the guise of "comfort dog." So, for kicks, I looked up, "What is a comfort dog?" There were many matches, including a link to a government report explaining the need for them and their purpose of providing comfort and support. Which got me thinking: Why exactly can't humans turn to their own species for this fulfillment? Then I looked up, "What is a comfort human?" Nothing. And so, Comfort Human™ was born. I would be the emotional support and comfort companion for those with Alzheimer's/dementia, and do so in person whenever I could, and create unique initiatives in the same vein for when in person wasn't an option, and on a large scale.

One project was Pen Palz, a one-sided pen pal program in which I mailed greeting cards to the same residents of memory-care facilities each month. The hundreds of handmade cards incorporated sensory elements, such as buttons and puffy balls, since touch therapy can be calming for them. Another project was the distribution of toy baby dolls to memory-care units during the 2020 Covid-19 pandemic to help with loneliness and lack of companionship while in quarantine isolation.

And the creative division of Comfort Human™ focuses on innovative ways to raise awareness through original content, such as this book.

Spend time around people with Alzheimer's/dementia and you'll notice certain things. That will likely include observing how family members and friends constantly repeat to their loved one, "Don't you remember?"

I'm going to give you a cold, hard fact: They probably don't remember. They probably never will. If they do, you might not be around to hear it.

If you already know this is a disease that affects memory, why are you trying to test their memory?

Since I rarely knew anything about my patients, our visits never ended in disappointment for me or for them because of something they couldn't recall. I figured out rather quickly that cocktail party small talk wasn't going to work with Alzheimer's/dementia. "What did you do for a living?" or "How many kids do you have?" often resulted in, "You know, I don't remember." Conversely, I might get a tall tale that their family would later tell me wasn't true.

It was one of my patients who got me thinking. She told me, "The mind might forget, but the heart does not." I don't know whether she was lucid with that statement, but it was really profound. And profoundly simple: Let feelings, not memories, lead the conversation when talking to someone with Alzheimer's/dementia. I decided to experiment with this idea by initially steering the conversation in the direction of a single topic: love. The heart does not forget. My line of questioning took on various forms, depending on each patient's stage of Alzheimer's/dementia. "How did you know you were in love?" "How do I know I've met the right man?" "What does love feel like?" "What made you decide to get married?" "How do I get a man to fall in love with me?" These were not memory questions. They required emotion and gut-based answers.

I found that they did not hesitate to respond and there was no pain on their face from knowing their recall had failed. What I got was pure gold—pontifications, opinions, unfiltered responses. And they enjoyed having a laugh and making me laugh. Patients were particularly outspoken when it came to "How do I find a boyfriend?" including "Men want boobs. They are sex animals and jackasses" and "Don't bother. Men are problems anyway." One inquired about where I'd been looking for men to date: "Do you go out socially? Like to dances?" On "How do I get men to like me?" I was told I needed to "put color in your hair," wear blush, but "not a lot," and that I needed "lipstick, like red or orange-red." It had to be red to get a guy? "Yes." I was receiving more solid advice than I'd ever seen in any women's magazines. One patient even began her advice with, "A lot of young women like you and me…."

Whether it was a resident who was new to the memory-care unit and I needed an icebreaker for our introduction, or someone I had already known for years through my volunteering, this simple conversational technique was working—and it was fun for both of us. I expanded to more topics, but always began with, "I need your help with something…." More often than not, that request alone perked them up. It gave them a purpose and they could see that someone wanted to listen, not talk at them.

Occasionally, I even sought their advice on actual situations I was in or that friends were dealing with, like the one who kept meeting men who were wrong for her: "Well, that's her problem—if she's in Frog Town, she'll find frogs." Another friend was getting married, so a patient and I together wrote a message in the card about love and marriage, and we both signed our names.

"How do I…", "How do you…", and "What should I…" are solid conversation starters as well. Nothing is off the table as long as it's not about giving them a pop quiz. Ask for help or ask for advice. Just ask something, anything, except for "Don't you remember?"

I once had a patient with the most advanced case of "word salad" I'd ever experienced. She was perky and very talkative, but the words coming out of her mouth were a complete jumble, mixed together randomly into a total mess. For example, as I was leaving after a visit, I said, "Have a good day!" and she enthusiastically replied, "Have a good napkin!" Yes, Alzheimer's/dementia does have its funny moments. Laughing doesn't make you insensitive; it makes you human. All conversations with her were like that, and could she ever talk! Never did I have any idea what our lengthy chats were about, and if I had ever responded to something she said with a completely unrelated answer, she never let on. But I always started us out of the gate with, "I need your help…" and away she went.

When patients couldn't speak or were hearing impaired, or English wasn't their first language, conversations would instead be written down or drawn.

I always carried a spiral notebook and pen so that we could "talk" or I could doodle pictures to represent words. I'm not an artist by any means, but they still managed to make enough sense of my work to remain engaged and present. It's why I felt compelled to draw my own illustrations that accompany certain quotes in this book. A full-circle kind of thing.

Conversations With Alzheimer's is a compilation of sage advice and honest truths about life, love, and aging, spoken by the people least expected to be capable of telling you how to live your best life.

I hope if nothing else, *Conversations With Alzheimer's* removes the stereotype that someone with Alzheimer's/dementia is incapable of partaking in a stimulating conversation. These pages are the most inspiring snippets of advice I have ever received in my life, and I continue to dish these same quotes out to friends and family today, always leading with, "A patient once told me…." Sharing their quotes is how I've been able to honor the incredible men and women who came into and left my life. To be able to share them with you keeps their spirit alive.

Alzheimer's/dementia robs us of much of the person we once knew. But if you can try to accept those difficult changes in their mental capacities and allow this "new" person to introduce themselves to you through these conversations, I guarantee you'll appreciate them just as much. I shouldn't be the only person enjoying conversations with your loved one!

Something else: Just because they forgot how to tell their stories doesn't mean you need to stop telling their stories. I had a patient explain, "When you get to be 98 years old, you have a lot of stories to tell. But you learn that once you're here." As in, it was now too late to share those memories.

I had a patient in a wheelchair who was only capable of making loud noises, not words, which disturbed other residents, so she was always relegated to the back of the group-activity room by herself. I didn't want her to feel alone, so every visit, I'd say hello. It took many visits before she stopped hitting me or looking away when she saw me coming. One day I held my ground: "I need your help…." She didn't respond, but she also was not combative. When I passed by her during my next visit, she reached her hand out for mine and then held it to her chest. The heart does not forget.

Her son flew in to visit a couple months later and was surprised to find his mother sitting and smiling with someone socially. He told me that she'd been in a concentration camp and that Nazis forced her and other women who were deemed beautiful to lie on the ground so that they could step on their faces and break their jaws to make them less attractive. She later went on to become an activist and would call the German embassy collect. Why? "You could afford gas," she told them. "You can afford my call."

Other stories shared with me about my patients:
- My mother danced with Mikhail Baryshnikov.
- My father was in the war and had been shot. He also taught himself Sanskrit.
- My aunt was the first woman on her city council.
- My father used to be a boxer.
- My uncle had been in charge of firing torpedoes at Pearl Harbor.
- My friend worked at a theater company when she was a teen and sold tap and ballet shoes and costumes. She used to make pasties for dancers.

- My father was an engineer for a railroad company and traveled all around the United States for work.
- My grandmother used to throw parties at her house for servicemen during the war.
- My sister taught second grade. They wouldn't let her teach first grade because she was left-handed.
- My mom met Franklin Delano Roosevelt on the street. She said, 'Hi.'

You can be their best storyteller when they can no longer tell their stories. But also, be ready for the new stories they're going to tell.

Tori Tellem

CHAPTER ONE
AGING

How old am I?

97.

Oh, that's old.

Why, how old do you feel?

97.

Grey hairs are honorable.

♡

I'm 90, but I could live another 100 years.
There's still so much I want to see and do.

♡

It's hard being old.
Especially for the ones who weren't clever.

♡

The key to being healthy at 95?
Eat everything on your plate.
And don't complain about food—ever.

*The only thing in life we have are our
memories. Memories and gall bladder.*

I was happy when I was 70.
I had a few dollars on me.

You won't forget, and I won't remember.

♡

I'm at a good age to think about things, remember things, and realize things.

♡

At my age, I want to be any age.

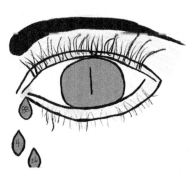

You bring years to my eyes.

When I die, I don't want the church thing.
Say a prayer and put me in the ground.
The rest is just a waste of time.

At my age I don't remember much.
You remember the nice things, not the rest.

I'll never grow up. I don't have time.

My favorite birthday?
50, because I couldn't believe
I made it that far.

♡

You remember everything,
or you remember nothing.

♡

I wish I could die. I'd be happier.

♡

We have the same things,
only mine are older.

How am I?
Upright and breathing.

My sister was 109.
I said to her,
'How long are you going to live?'

If you're over 40 and your career isn't
happening, it's time to give up.

I've been better, but it costs more.

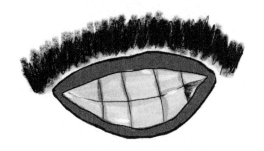

I need glasses and some teeth pulled,
but should I bother if I'm going to die?

♡

You're not getting older. You're old.

♡

You know what they call me here?
'Babyface.'
I'm 95, but I don't look it.

Do I feel 90? No.
But that's because I don't associate
something negative to it. It's not fair to
life if you feel that way about life.

I think what I'll remember most about
these years is how I didn't believe in this
enough to fight for it at the end.

I have some regrets, but they aren't big.
More like, why did I do it that way,
or why didn't I do it sooner?

CHAPTER TWO
LOVE

Are you married?

No.

That's OK. You look fine.

What's not romantic isn't right.

♡

Tying the knot?
What they don't tell you is it's a slipknot.

♡

Marriage is when you want to be happy
and you want someone else to be happy.

♡

Did I fall in love
with my husband right away?
Oh, yes. No un-falling.

Marriage is good for maybe the first day
you get married.
After that you can go throw it in the lake.

♡

They are marriage vows,
not marriage wows.

♡

Marriage isn't thrills. It's chills.

♡

I haven't experienced love much.
I think there is a special code.

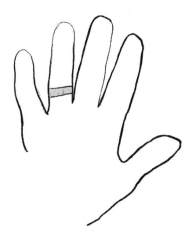

I was married 40 years.
The secret to a long marriage?
'Yes, darling.'

My father swept my mother off her feet.
He grabbed her so no one else could.

The secret to love: Be truthful.

Every morning my husband said,
'You are so beautiful and I love you
and I can't believe how lucky I am.'
We married when I was 19
and he died when I was 34,
but he said it to me every single day,
how ever many years
there are between 19 and 34.

Act like a lady and you will attract a
gentleman.

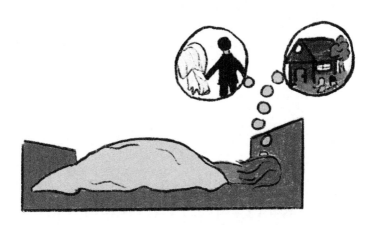

When I can't sleep at night,
I think about our romance.

He was easy on the eyes,
but also easy on the heart.

Love is a problem if you become
engulfed. I've managed to keep the wolf
at the door.

My family all loved each other.
Love is all I know. I was born into it,
I lived it, and I will go out that way.

I never got married again because once
you've had the best, you can't settle.
I knew I'd never find anyone who lived up
to his standards.

*When I met my husband, he was
brilliant and artistic and funny,
and I fell in love right away and held on.*

♡

What's a 'real man'? If I knew, I would
keep him for myself.

Marriage is when you're talking to
someone who is a stranger to you.

♡

My husband wasn't good with pen and
paper. He was better at talking.
Like when he said, 'Let's get married,'
I did after six weeks.

♡

My wife and I weren't inseparable.
We were invincible.

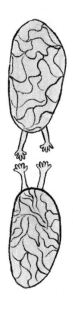

Marriage is difficult—
two minds thinking one way.

♡

If you want more than a 'normal' woman,
you're going to have to work for it.

On first impression, you look happy.

♡

We got married in Vegas and rented a house that night. I bought coffee cake and made coffee and I called that a wedding cake. Then we had our sex.

♡

When he died, I wanted to go with him.

♡

He keeps talking like that, no one will want to live with him.

My husband died when he was very
young, like maybe 50.
It was hard. It's hard when you love,
it's easy when you don't.

My sister's husband was the homeliest
man you've ever laid eyes on.
He was tall, skinny, buck teeth,
and thick glasses,
but he treated her like a queen.

Love and dancing are all the same.
You just want to stay upright and not
land on your head.

The women all had reasons to divorce me
before I could marry them.

♡

In my estimation, there is no 'real man'.
Maybe in looks, but once you talk to him,
forget it. I don't think there is anyone
'real' today.

♡

I'm not sure it's in me
to make bells ring for any man.

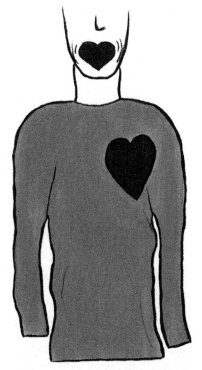

CHAPTER THREE
LIFE

I don't care how I look in coats. It's about keeping my body comfortable and not whether I have a nice body, although I assume I have a nice body.

Smile from your heart, not your gut.

The lesson in life is to be around people
who make you feel good.
That's what I learned.

Life has a way of changing people.
People don't have a way of changing life.

After I cry, my face is super salty.

I knew a woman who never laughed.
It was easier to make a prune smile.

I'm so hungry, I could eat a horse.
But first, I would like its hooves removed.

Tears will come, but never dry.

Don't take life too seriously,
but you can't leave it off either.

*We all have such different lives.
I don't know if that's a good thing.*

♡

I know you're a girl, but you can do
anything that you really, really, really
want to do.

I don't know how good of a life it was,
but good memories.

Got my dad's tall side and
my mom's big mouth.

Life is normal. Normal of sorts.

There is no good and bad,
only good and indifferent.

Aside from a dog and cat,
I know nothing about animals.

♡

Some women dress to the nines.
I dress to the twos.

♡

I don't get these guys with their beards.

*A person is a person whether
they are from New York,
Los Angeles, or Australia.*

Happy is where you find it.

*The whole world wants to smile,
but they don't know how.*

♡

People know their limits. When
something's hot, you drop it.

Living isn't easy.

Everyone says the mother
is always harder than the father.

I like many things, but not everything.

What would I do with
a million dollars?
I'd have no problem getting rid of it.

We all have a book with us.
It's in our head.

I don't need a lot to be happy.
I don't want the whole barrel.

I like everything about me.

No one knows how much you cry.

The bad things in life?
They're never really that bad.

I'm just not good with people
I don't already like.

CHAPTER FOUR
WISDOM

Dad always said,

'Try not to do anything stupid.'

He was trying to be funny, but he

was right. Ask yourself if what you

want to do is intelligent or stupid.

A man goes into the forest for peace
and comes out with a thought.

One never knows the answer.

When things are vague, it's because
something hurt you then.

Laughter is always a good way to go.
Good friends also help.

Follow the raindrops.

You do what you have to do,
then you don't worry about it.

Don't take the results before they happen.

♡

You have to try a whole lot of things
before you know
what you don't want to do.

♡

You take care and clean your car good.

♡

What was bothering you last week you
probably can't remember.
Same with what's bothering you now.

You want to insult a smoker?
Call them 'Smokerface.'

Talk to yourself.

When I have nothing to do,
I daydream about my life.

I can't give advice because I'm not an
advisor person. I only tell what I know.

If you don't have anything,
you can at least have fun.

♡

In pictures, reindeer look nice. But in person, they have horns and will kill you.

*If you're a lazy person,
you'll give birth to a boy.*

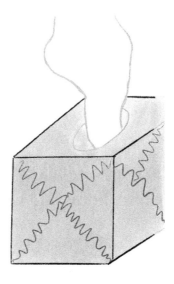

*If you want someone to stop crying,
offer them a tissue.*

♡

Have the day you have.

It's nice what you want,
and it's nice what you get.

By being hurt, you're only hurting
yourself.

Don't concentrate on what will happen.
Concentrate on now.

Go ahead and complain. It won't help.

*Here's the secret that no one knows
for taking pills: They all try to swallow
them with a big gulp of water.
You have to swish them around in your
mouth a bit to lubricate them.
Then they go right down.*

In order to be quiet, you have to be noisy.
In order to be lucky, you have to be smart.

Comb your hair three times a day and you will have a wonderful life.

I need a writer to tell a story, about someone who is able to do anything they want in life simply by having the emotional belief that they can.

Every night I look east. That's where the future is. You won't get everything you see, but you'll get close.

Never regret what you could have done.

♡

We can only hope from today until
tomorrow.

♡

It's time to say goodnight.
It's time to close up the shop.

THE END